solutions

GOVERNC

CW01068523

Financial Management

Robin Hammerton

© pfp publishing limited 2002

First published in Britain in 2002 by
pfp publishing limited
61 Gray's Inn Road
London WC1X 8TH

Author Robin Hammerton
Series editor Lynn Cousins
Editor Michael Coveney
Design Christine Cox
Illustrations David Farris

Printed and bound in the UK.

A catalogue record for this book is available from the
British Library.

ISBN 1 874050 73 2

Other books in this series
• *Your Budget* ISBN 1 874050 74 0
• *Raising Additional Income* ISBN 1 874050 72 4

pfp orders and customer service
Tel: 0870 241 0731
Web: www.pfp-publishing.com

solutions Financial Management

Contents

Summary

The big picture

The law gives schools delegated budgets, which have to cover virtually all their running costs. This is good. Headteachers, governors and staff are trusted to make financial decisions because they know what's needed on the ground. Schools' budget freedom is very precious because it gives the people closest to the action the financial clout to make their plans come to life.

However, no one says that having financial autonomy is easy – quite the opposite. Headteachers are leading educators, not accountants. Some governors may have good financial skills but it's not their role to micromanage the school accounts, even if they have the time.

So there are some clear issues. Who does what? How do we make sure that managing the budget is about achieving the best educational outcomes for children, not just balancing the books? What financial procedures and routines are needed? How do we satisfy the need for accountability?

Tackling the problem

This book is not a dry financial manual. It's actually about getting results for children. The key issues concern using and targeting money to support learning, and schools having confidence in their own financial judgement.

There's a section on how to properly and effectively involve different groups of people – governors, teachers and support staff – in budget management. This is followed by practical guidance on how to use the main delegated budget alongside devolved capital money, the Standards Fund and voluntary funds to achieve the outcomes you want. The book then explains how to monitor expenditure effectively and what to do as a result. It outlines what needs to be done to manage finances well from day to day. Finally, it looks at how to evaluate the impact on pupils of financial decisions, use comparative information and prepare for audit.

The text is written sympathetically from the head's point of view. But it doesn't duck the difficult questions we often have to ask ourselves. The book is about using money to achieve high standards for children after all. However, it always offers answers, or points clearly to where they can be found.

The book reflects current practice in Best Value and Consistent Financial Reporting (CFR).

CHAPTER 1

What is the legal position about school finances?

The law about school finances is generally supportive to schools. It recognises that those of us who work at the chalkface are best placed to make the strategic decisions, underpinned by running the budget. The law gives us precious freedoms and rights to make the best decisions for our pupils.

If we're going to think about the best ways of managing our school finances, the legal framework is a surprisingly positive place to begin.

You need to know

1 what the purpose is, legally, of the school budget

2 who owns the money in the school bank account

3 your partnership role in budget management

1 The legal purpose of the school budget.

Money is given to schools so that they can educate their pupils. So in law the budget must be spent on the purposes of the school. It has to cover almost all the expenses of running the school including staffing costs. But there's more going on than this.

Since 1988 government policy has been firmly that schools should run their own financial affairs. This gives schools the monetary clout to back up their educational decisions. (Colleagues in other countries often view this with envy.) It provides the means by which we can shape children's everyday experiences by making good choices about resourcing – physical and human.

It also brings accountability – there's no one else (such as the LEA) to blame, or to take the credit! This book and others in the *Solutions* series look at key ways of making the system work well.

> Having control of your budget – however small it is – gives you much broader management freedom.

2 Some important legal principles which underpin the ownership of the money in the school bank account.

The LEA has a duty in law to have a scheme for funding all its schools. There's more about how this works in Chapter 2. Rather than hold the school budget funds centrally, the LEA must give them to the schools and allow them to run their own bank accounts. However, in strict legal terms, money in school bank accounts still belongs to the local authority and not to the schools, so all the money you spend in school has to be accounted for by the authority. That's one of the reasons why it has to be managed well.

Let's look at four important principles in more depth.

Delegation

This is the vital point. Your school budget may formally belong to the LEA but legally it's yours to spend. Delegation means delegation. As long as you use the money

- in good faith

- in the interests of your pupils

- within the law and LEA regulations

and you manage things well, there's very little the LEA can do to intervene. It's your call.

> The law considers that you're best placed to make the financial decisions for your school, so if you're ever questioned don't be afraid to stick to your guns.

However, it's important to bear in mind that in law the budget is delegated to the governors, not the head. The financial decisions you take, therefore, need to be within the context of school policy and the limits you've agreed with your governors. Governors will certainly need to work with you to set and then agree the budget plan at the start of the financial year and help you to monitor spending as the year goes on. The full governing body must agree the final budget plan each year. There's more about this in Chapters 3 and 7.

Suspension

We don't want to dwell on this but it's helpful to be clear that in law an LEA may suspend the delegation of a school budget if the governing body has

- 'persistently or substantially' not complied with delegation requirements

- not managed the delegated budget satisfactorily.

In these circumstances the LEA would run the school's finances for the period of the suspension. However, suspension is rare and

can be appealed against to the Secretary of State. One month's warning of suspension must normally be given and the LEA must provide detailed written reasons for its decision.

> An LEA cannot suspend delegation because it doesn't agree with how the school is spending its money. There has to be clear mismanagement.

If a school overspends and goes into deficit – effectively borrowing from the LEA – delegation will not necessarily be withdrawn. However, it will probably be necessary for the governing body to agree a plan with the authority to repay the shortfall over time.

Charging and other income

Your school is normally allowed to keep income from activities such as

- lettings

- fundraising activities

- voluntary contributions

- sale of assets.

Of course, this income has to be spent on the purposes of the school.

Legally, in a state school you have to provide education free to your pupils. While there is no restriction on seeking voluntary contributions – as long as these are truly voluntary – you can only impose charges on parents in limited circumstances such as

- board and lodging on residential visits

- individual music lessons

- activities partly or mainly out of school hours.

These charges must be fair and you need to have a charging policy so that everyone knows where they stand.

Account balances

Money delegated by the LEA stays with the school if not spent by the end of the financial year. This enables you to save up for big projects or planned future needs and is a great freedom. However it's unwise to allow excessive reserves to build up as this

- may not be fair to the pupils currently on roll

- might give the appearance that you have more money than you know what do with.

Keeping 3–5% of your annual budget in reserve is probably about right, unless you require more for clearly identified needs.

> Keeping hold of unspent money is an important legal freedom. You can safeguard this by clearly earmarking your reserves for specific future expenditure.

3 Ideas to help you and your governors build a strong partnership in budget management.

We've already seen that budgets are delegated to the governing body, not the headteacher. In law it's down to the governing body to

- decide how to spend the delegated budget

- respond to consultation about changes to the LEA's scheme of funding schools

- ensure that accurate records are kept.

Of course, governors can delegate much of this to the headteacher. Good practice demands this. It's essential to establish an attitude of partnership.

The box opposite describes a common trap which can happen when an individual governor – however well-intentioned and highly qualified – is allowed to be the sole governor representative on financial matters.

By following the advice overleaf you can avoid such pitfalls and develop a productive working relationship with your governors.

Avoid this trap

Fred, a chartered accountant, is a respected member of the community and new to the governing body. He seems the natural choice to chair the finance committee and oversee the school budget. He takes this role very seriously and is committed to helping the school. Angela, the head, is initially very keen to work with Fred and they build slots into their busy diaries to work together. As time progresses, however, both parties find things difficult. Angela feels that Fred is insufficiently understanding of the school's educational needs. She has to spend too long justifying potential expenditure to him and this is slowing down progress in important areas as well as wearing her out. Although he clearly means well, he doesn't seem to understand that schools are about children and learning and not just the bottom line of the accounts. Fred feels that Angela is inclined to want to do things without agreeing them with him. He only wants to help. He is surprised and a little hurt that she is becoming so reluctant to use his expertise – he is a financial specialist after all. And surely the law is on his side – isn't finance a matter for the governors?

Here's a checklist to help you build a good partnership with your governors over financial management that satisfies the letter and spirit of the law.

- Make sure that you value the expertise and wisdom governors may contribute to corporate decision-making about strategy and how the finance relates to it (this can be a fantastic support to you). In return you can expect them to value the professional expertise that you bring to these discussions.

- Ensure that there is a distinction between strategic and day-to-day management of the finances. As with all aspects of school life, governors should only be involved in the former.

- Make sure you give good, accurate, clear information to governors about finance and spending options when needed. This enables them to do what the law requires, shows them you know what you're doing, and will help you to gain their trust.

- Try not to allow any individual governor, however competent and helpful, to become solely responsible for finances. Governing bodies are corporate entities.

- As a competent head, working with your LEA and finance officer, you have enough expertise to manage the budget. This doesn't mean that financially qualified governors can't be a great help – they can – but it's right to expect your governors to trust you to run the finances for them day

to day and to make good decisions about spending to meet the agreed strategic priorities.

- Be patient but persistent if the partnership takes time to build fully.

In summary

Managing your own school finance is a vital, cherished opportunity given by the law for very good reasons. Enjoy the possibilities it brings and use them to benefit the people who count – your pupils.

▶ **Next step**

Make sure you have clear ground rules established about who does what in your school's financial management. In Chapter 3 we'll look in more detail at the roles that need to be played.

CHAPTER 2

Where does the money come from?

To manage our budget well, it's helpful to understand where the money comes from, how it gets to us and how we might be able to influence the process. There are few things as complex as local authority finance and luckily we don't have to know all the ins and outs.

This chapter is a summary of the main points. You will find more detail on where your budget comes from in Steve Mynard's book *Solutions: Your Budget* in this series.

You need to

1 **understand how your school budget is decided**

2 **consider responding to LEA consultations**

3 **check that your budget is correct**

4 **make use of your Section 52 statement**

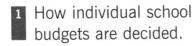 How individual school budgets are decided.

In a nutshell, the process works like this.

The local authority arranges its overall budget

The local authority determines its overall budget for all the services it provides. This is complex as there are many rules and regulations that have to be adhered to.

It then decides how much of this will be given to education. Within this, the lion's share has to be allocated to the provision of school education, known as the Local Schools' Budget (LSB).

Most of this will be delegated to schools but the LEA will keep a percentage for its central work.

Money is delegated to schools using a formula

The LEA has to have a formula to decide how much money each school receives – the Individual School Budget (ISB). This has to be based mainly on the number of pupils in the school.

Children in different year groups are often funded differently. Generally (and somewhat controversially) secondary pupils receive more funding than those in primary schools for example.

Other factors that can be in the formula include

- Special Educational Needs

- measures of socio-economic factors or social deprivation

- the nature and size of each school's buildings and grounds

- support for small schools.

From this it can be seen that schools of similar size or type may receive quite different budgets even within the same LEA. Between LEAs, there can be even greater differences. No wonder there is a clamour for a national formula from schools that seem to lose out.

> **If part of your budget is decided by a future pupil number estimate, it's usually sensible to be cautious in your estimate to avoid a clawback. This can happen if your actual pupil numbers are not as high as you predicted.**

2 Responding to LEA consultations.

Each year your LEA must consult with you and your governing body about its delegation scheme for the following year. Among all the consultations we receive, this one can be well worth spending the time on. Within LEAs there are also consultation groups often known as Schools Forums.

Here are some of the points you may wish to consider.

Special needs funding

Is the funding for SEN based on actual needs or on other measures, such as socio-economic factors or test results? Is this fair? What are the implications for the children in your school?

Pupil mobility

Are there good arrangements for helping and protecting schools that may have sudden and unpredictable changes in pupil numbers – perhaps because of traveller children, a military base or changing social circumstances?

Small and large schools

How effective is the formula in providing for the needs of schools of all sizes?

Differences in Age Weighted Pupil Unit

How does the LEA justify any differences in funding given to pupils in different year groups? Are the reasons given justified or perhaps based too much on historic factors?

Factors specific to your school

Are there any areas in which your school has genuine, specific needs for which the formula does not provide?

The good points

Finally, give praise where it's due. It's thoughtful, as well as shrewd, to point out areas where the LEA's formula is working well and is helping to bring about good educational outcomes.

> Your views may carry more weight if they are not based just on the parochial interest of your own school. Points made by groups of schools together can be very powerful.

3 Check your budget.

Like everyone else, LEAs can make genuine mistakes and it is worth checking your budget. In practice this is likely to mean three things.

- Check the arithmetic in any budget statements sent to you.

- Verify that whatever you're entitled to in the formula actually appears in the budget you're given.

- Make sure that the actual transfers of money from the LEA into your school's bank account are correct.

4 Make use of your Section 52 statement.

After the end of each financial year your LEA must produce a financial out-turn statement, known as the Section 52 statement, which should come to your school.

The statement will be a list, probably in booklet form, of financial facts and figures. On the face of it, it's not the most enticing read. Yet if you take time to make sense of the tables, it provides information that can be helpful. It tells you

- what the LEA has spent centrally

- the ISB and Standards Fund amount given to each school

- how much each school has spent

- the rollover (balance carried forward) for each school in actual and percentage terms.

This gives you an opportunity to compare what you're doing with other schools and to see how your budget matches up to theirs.

In summary

It's worth knowing about the process that takes place to get money into school. Use your knowledge to check that you're receiving what you're entitled to and to make your views known about the LEA's financial scheme if you need to.

▶ **Next step**

Consider benchmarking the way you use your school budget against other schools. There's more about this in Chapter 13.

CHAPTER 3

Who should be doing what in financial management?

In Chapter 1 we saw that the school budget is legally delegated to the governing body. As head you will have a pivotal role in helping the governors with their responsibilities and in making a number of decisions on their behalf. We saw the kinds of problems that might occur if the partnership between head and governors doesn't work well or there aren't clear, workable ground rules about the roles people play. Additionally, you don't have time to do it all and it's good to involve others. So you'll need to share the financial workload with your staff.

There are few hard and fast rules about exactly how this demarcation should work. Each school needs to agree its own policy. However, this chapter outlines a model of who might do what. You, your governors and staff might find it handy to use and adapt for your own purposes.

You need to

1 delegate financial responsibilities

2 make practical arrangements for financial administration by support staff

3 ensure that budget holders, such as curriculum leaders, know what's expected of them

1 Through discussions with your governors decide the particular financial responsibilities of governors, head and senior staff.

It's important to get this right and to review these responsibilities from time to time.

> It's helpful, not to say essential, to have a clear, written finance policy.

Guidance will be available from your LEA about good financial procedures, ensuring propriety and proper checks and balances. It's important to take full account of this. But the real decisions you have to take in school are

- who does what

- the limits of authority.

The table opposite shows a model of how responsibilities can be helpfully split.

> If you have a computerised management information system (MIS) it will help to reduce the workload for you and your admin officer. If you are reviewing or looking for an MIS, use the checklist on page 79 to help you choose one that suits your needs.

2 Practical arrangements for financial administration by support staff.

It's not the best use of your time to become bogged down in financial administration. Day-to-day work is ideally done by a member of the support staff. If possible, budget for sufficient time and training for a secretary, bursar or finance officer to carry out these tasks.

- Day-to-day administration of the school's delegated budget, Standards Fund and capital funding.

- Providing financial reports for head, staff and governors.

- Checking that the correct sums of money arrive in the school bank account from the LEA.

- Ensuring payroll information is accurate.

- Operating the school's main bank account and reconciling statements.

- Raising and managing orders.

- Paying authorised invoices.

- Banking school income.

- Being responsible for the day-to-day operation of other accounts and monies used in school (for instance a school

Headteacher/senior staff	Governors (usually through the finance committee, or equivalent)
● Prepare a budget each year, based on the school's strategic needs shown in the SIP.	● Approve the budget each year, ensuring that its priorities reflect the school's strategic aims (this must be done by the full governing body, though more detailed preliminary work can be done in a committee).
● Keep up to date with LEA and national finance policies and schemes.	
● Give necessary advice and encouragement to the governing body.	● Support the head in preparing the budget (this is best done by a very small group or the finance committee chair).
● Ensure the provision of clear financial reports to governors – explain any changes and their implications as the financial year progresses.	● Monitor the budget during the financial year with the head; support the head in ensuring the budget is meeting strategic aims in practice and that the children are getting the planned benefits.
● Ensure that the school is getting good value for the money it spends and the pupils are benefiting as they should.	
● Make budget holders accountable for their spending decisions.	● Make any necessary significant budget or strategic changes during the year on the head's recommendation (this could result from an unforeseen change in staffing needs for example).
● Work closely with support staff who administer the school's finance, supporting and ensuring the work is being carried out efficiently.	
● Ensure that financial procedures and policies are followed.	● With the head, ensure that suitable financial procedures and policies are in place.
● Make most virements and budget adjustments during the year, based on strategic needs.	● Make larger virements (over a determined amount) usually on recommendation of the head.

voluntary fund, school journey account, dinner money, any funds pupils have raised for charity, or payments for items such as school photographs).

A good finance officer builds up considerable experience and expertise. Give him or her scope to use these skills and put ideas into practice.

In summary

In a well-run school the governing body and head have complementary responsibilities for management of the finances that they've agreed together. They encourage and rely on each other. In turn, the head ensures that the support he or she needs from staff members is organised and the people involved know what is expected.

3 Ensure that budget holders know what is expected of them.

You'll probably allocate sums of money to members of staff with specific duties –such as curriculum leaders – to spend in developing their area of responsibility. These allocations of school money are amongst those that can make the most impact on children's learning, as they directly support the curriculum. The most important financial duties these staff are likely to have are

• preparing bids

• spending the allocated budget effectively to achieve the desired outcomes for pupils

• straightforward reporting or accounting for the expenditure.

It's important this work is done well and we'll explore it in more detail in the next chapter.

▶ **Next step**

Look in more depth at how you can involve senior staff and budget holders in financial management. Consider ways of developing their skills and understanding. For ideas on ways to involve your staff see Chapter 4.

CHAPTER 4

How do I involve other staff in the budget?

Teachers are happy to have money to spend on their areas of responsibility but beyond this they may have little enthusiasm for setting budgets and managing finances. They are, after all, teachers not accountants and this attitude is quite understandable.

However, for senior staff especially it can be very useful, and a wise career move, to get involved in the management of finance. We've seen that financial freedom helps to underpin wider management freedom. Staff with middle or senior management responsibilities can support their own professional development through experience of financial management, as well as having some input into financial decisions within the school.

You need to

1 involve appropriate staff in managing the finances

2 give responsibility and accountability to staff who hold budgets

3 have a financial process which ensures honesty and transparency

1 Ways of involving staff in managing the finances.

Share the big picture

When you're working on budget issues, share what's happening and what's in your mind with your senior team. Let them know briefly about

- how the school budget is prepared

- all the different types of expenditure that need to be included

- any cutback or additional funding that is having an effect

- choices that have to be made (it's good, of course, to involve and consult senior staff when to make these choices)

- how the budget is supporting SIP priorities.

This will help them to see more clearly how the big picture is made up and the kinds of issues that you and the governors have to address. In turn, this should enable them to

- help you in your work on budget management

- support you by explaining to other staff why particular financial decisions or actions have been taken.

Allow people to run parts of the budget

You, as head, are responsible for running the budget day to day. However, there's no reason to do all the work by yourself. You're responsible, too, for the standard of all the teaching but you don't do all of that! Give your senior people some responsibility.

How you do this will depend greatly on the size and circumstances of your school, and the stage of development of your staff. You'll also need to give some explanations, or arrange some training, so that everyone knows what is expected.

> **If you give senior colleagues responsibility to manage parts of the school budget, you'll develop their role and perhaps allow yourself to spend more time focusing on the curriculum.**

Consider delegating the management of the following budget headings to other staff.

Curriculum

This is the most frequently delegated. Almost all schools give budgets to each curriculum leader to spend on resources for the subject. This is often related to a subject development plan or similar.

You may decide how much money every subject receives or you could set an overall sum for the whole curriculum and then delegate the allocation of amounts for each subject to a senior teacher. This may be particularly valuable if you have a designated curriculum manager, who would then monitor individual subject spending during the year.

Continuing professional development

Running the CPD budget (whether it's from the Standards Fund or your delegated budget) can be a very good opportunity for a suitable teacher.

This may involve managing the costs of courses and other training opportunities as well as the supply expenditure when people are released. It will give the person freedom to make real choices about the INSET priorities for the school.

Sickness supply

It can be a very good idea to delegate the sickness supply budget to someone else. This particularly applies if you have a senior person, say a deputy, who is in charge of making sure that all classes are covered each day. This will give that person both the autonomy and the accountability for the decisions they take.

Key stage/departmental and SATs cover

You may provide individual budgets for key stages or departments. These could include the money allocated for supply cover for SATs. This gives your staff the freedom and accountability to plan things as they see fit.

Newly qualified teachers

If you have a newly qualified teacher in your school, you'll receive specific funding in the Standards Fund to pay supply costs for the 0.1 release time they're entitled to. This time can be used flexibly to help the NQT to develop. To make the most of this it might be helpful to give responsibility for looking after the funding to the NQT's mentor.

Buildings and capital projects

Many schools allow caretakers or site managers to run appropriate budgets for maintenance and for basic provisions such as soap and toilet rolls. This can be extended so that the site manager takes much greater responsibility for handling funds for building works and devolved capital projects (more about this in Chapter 6).

Standards Fund

When the Standards Fund and its predecessors were only concerned with staff training, some heads chose to delegate managing this area to a senior colleague. However, the fund is now much more complex and supplements other school spending in a variety of areas. Consequently, it has become tricky for someone to manage as a discrete whole and it is not really a good idea to delegate the management of this budget heading.

See Chapter 5 for more detail about the Standards Fund.

2 Give responsibility and accountability to budget holders.

When you give control of part of the school budget to someone else, it's important to

- discuss and agree with them what the educational or other objectives of spending that money are

- allow the person freedom to manage the budget on a day-to-day basis without interference

- monitor with them how effectively the budget is being managed and used

- assess with them, at the end of the financial year, whether the original targets have been achieved.

> When you delegate financial control to members of staff, you're not just giving them the chance to spend money. By giving them the budget, you're giving them the responsibility of achieving outcomes they and you have determined.

3 A financial process to ensure honesty and transparency.

Most LEAs advise a straightforward system for ordering supplies, something like this.

Step 1

The budget holder decides on a purchase.

Step 2

The budget holder fills out a school order form for the purpose.

Step 3

The head (or other designated senior person) signs the order to authorise it.

Step 4

The finance officer processes and sends the order to the supplier.

Step 5

The supplier sends the item purchased to the school with an invoice.

Step 6

A nominated person in the school (often a secretary or caretaker) checks that what has been sent by the supplier is correct and intact.

Step 7

The finance officer organises a cheque for payment of the invoice, signs it, and keeps appropriate records.

Step 8

A designated person (not the one in Step 3) countersigns the cheque, which is sent to the supplier.

Step 9

The item is used to achieve the intended outcome.

This kind of system gives openness and allows for reasonable checks and balances throughout the process.

Discuss this with your staff, making sure that they understand the reasons why a number of people are involved at different stages and why they must keep strictly to the process. Set up your version of this process, putting in the names of the people rather than just the job titles to prevent any mistakes or short cuts.

In summary

You can develop your staff and your school by allowing others to share in the freedoms given by budget management. Make sure when you do this that people know what is expected of them and that they are responsible for the outcomes of financial decisions they take.

▶ Next step

Make sure your School Improvement Plan links finance to learning targets and that you are monitoring how well this works, in straightforward but effective ways. For more details see Chapter 9.

CHAPTER What do I do about managing the Standards Fund?

Money is power and most of the LEA's education budget is delegated to schools in their budgets. It's not surprising, therefore, that central government chooses to keep some cash back to invest solely in its own initiatives and priorities. This is what the Standards Fund is for. LEAs bid for Standards Fund money each year and have to make their own contribution to it. Most of the money they receive is then devolved to schools, in addition to and alongside the main school budget. The Standards Fund money has to be spent on specific, defined areas.

In recent years key aspects of government policy have included

- the national literacy and numeracy strategies

- increasing the number of teaching assistants

- school security

- social inclusion

- staff and governor training (incidentally, the sole purpose of the Standards Fund's predecessors – LEATG, GRIST and GEST)

- performance management

- infant class size reduction.

These and many other projects have been funded in schools through the Standards Fund.

At the same time many schools have requested

- more flexibility in how they can use the Standards Fund

- more simplicity in its operation.

As a result of this some changes have been made. It's a matter of opinion how effective these have been.

You need to

1 **check the rules on using Standards Fund money**

2 **with your governors, use the Standards Fund in the way that supports your school priorities best**

Check the rules.

Accounting

The Standards Fund has to be accounted for separately from the main school budget, even though the money usually arrives in the school bank account along with the main budget. This can make the whole business seem disproportionately complicated and time-consuming even though, under Consistent Financial Reporting (CFR), the respective budget headings are very clear. LEAs have different ways that they like us to explain our Standards Fund expenditure, so it's important to follow what's expected in your area. Whatever the case, your LEA should not impose undue bureaucracy on your school (for example by asking you to justify Standards Fund expenditure to an unreasonable degree).

Categories

Standards Fund money is allocated to your school under (currently) six main headings, with several sub-headings. These are set by the government. Many of them may be 'consolidated' to give you choice in how you allocate the money between them. You should receive very clear guidance from your LEA as to what you can and cannot do with the money under each heading. Information is also available on the DfES website, www.standards.dfes.gov.uk. It's sensible to read this carefully. However, be resourceful and imaginative when you do so, as it's often possible to use the money correctly in ways you might not immediately expect but which are right for your school. See section 2, overleaf.

> Standards Fund rules inevitably change from year to year. Check the changes as early as you can so that you can be proactive in using the money in the best way for your school.

Virements

A big concession given to schools by the government is the freedom to move money around between many of the Standards Fund headings. This can be done at the start of or during the financial year. It means that you can establish your own priorities rather than feeling compelled to spend money on something you might not really need. Be careful to check each year where virements are and are not permitted.

See Chapter 10 for more about the purpose and management of virements.

Rollover

It's important to check whether it'll be possible to roll over Standards Fund money from one financial year to the next, or whether it'll be taken back if unspent. Usually it can be kept until the August after the end of the financial year in which it was originally given. Use it before you lose it.

2 With your governors, use the Standards Fund to support your school priorities.

Manage the standards fund alongside your main budget

When you're setting and monitoring your main budget, include the Standards Fund in the process. Even though the formal accounting is separate, all the money in your school, wherever it comes from, is for the same purpose – educating your pupils. So in your mind, if not on the spreadsheets, it's good to blur the distinction.

For example, if you've chosen to employ teaching assistants by using Standards Fund money try not to think of them as 'Standards Fund assistants'. Rather, think of and use the fund as a reinforcement of your main budget expenditure.

For more information about budget monitoring, see Chapters 8 and 9.

> Your financial management is likely to be most coherent and efficient if you look on the Standards Fund as integral to your school finance as a whole. It's not best seen as an add-on. Joined-up thinking is the name of the game.

Use the standards fund correctly for your priorities

You'll have a number of needs for expenditure in your school. Maybe you want to provide some additional extra-curricular activities, organise some specific CPD, buy some equipment or increase staffing. When you check the categories, you'll almost certainly find that you can do, or support, many of these things with the Standards Fund. This is good management because it means you'll be matching government priorities to yours in the way that you consider is best for your school. This is likely to lead to better outcomes and allow you to spend your main budget on other important areas.

In summary

The Standards Fund is useful money, with restrictions. To manage it most effectively, carefully link the purposes the government says it must be spent on with your school priorities. Then plan and monitor Standards Fund expenditure closely with your main delegated budget.

▶ Next step

Consider how other pockets of money you have available, such as the School Fund, can be managed correctly and effectively. This is covered in Chapter 7.

CHAPTER 6

How do I deal with money devolved for capital expenditure?

In recent years the government has been determined to do something about the poor state of some school premises and generally to invest in buildings and infrastructure. As a result, schools receive a sum of money each year, known as Devolved Formula Capital, on top of the core budget. This chapter is about how to manage this money effectively and link it to other funding sources.

You need to

1 understand the basics

2 produce an Asset Management Plan

3 identify all sources of funding

4 manage capital projects efficiently

1 The basics of Devolved Formula Capital.

Frequently asked questions

■ **How is the devolved capital grant for each school decided?**

Using a formula, based mainly on pupil numbers.

■ **What can the money be spent on?**

Capital improvements to buildings. Examples would be

- extensions and conversions

- refurbishment

- improvements to support teaching and learning

- new windows

- ICT infrastructure such as cabling or suites (but not the computers themselves)

- health and safety works.

■ **What can't it be used for?**

You can't spend the money on repairs, maintenance or any equipment. However, sometimes the distinction between capital improvements and repairs and maintenance can be a grey area.

If you're not sure about a job in your school it can be well worth checking up and, if necessary, arguing your case.

■ **Can the capital money be rolled over or saved?**

Yes it can, for up to three years to pay for larger projects.

RIGHT, THAT'S 1500 PUPILS, WHICH MAKES. . .YES, ENOUGH DEVOLVED CAPITAL FOR A NEW ICT SUITE, LIBRARY AND GYMNASIUM!

▮ Do all schools receive the money?

Yes – all state schools apart from those in buildings less than three years old, who are assumed not to need it.

▮ Does the money come into the school bank account?

Usually, yes. However, like the Standards Fund (Chapter 5) it needs to be accounted for separately. The exceptions to this are voluntary aided schools, who are funded on the same basis but using a different mechanism. There's a special section for these schools at the end of this chapter.

2 Producing an Asset Management Plan.

Working with your governors, you need to produce an Asset Management Plan. You might not call it this, of course. It might be known as a Premises Development Plan or by various other names. The components, however, will be similar.

The Asset Management Plan should

- be part of your overall strategic improvement plan and related to other parts of it. For example, the development of a new computer suite is likely to link to your plan for staff training in ICT. The refurbishment of a library may link up with a book week and boosting the funds available for new purchases

- relate to the needs identified in the Condition Survey for your school, carried out periodically by your LEA, and any other surveys that have been done

- be flexible enough to meet changing needs, not set in stone

- draw upon finances available from various sources, not only devolved capital (see overleaf).

What is an Asset Management Plan?

Your Asset Management Plan could be produced in many formats but the basic elements should be

- a list of development works of all types planned for the school premises, including repairs, improvements and any major capital projects

- a broad costing for each work planned

- a timescale for each of the works, in a logical order, organised so that the funds should be available for each project at the time it is planned.

The plan is likely to cover a period of three years or more.

---

3 Identifying different sources of funding.

Devolved Formula Capital is a very useful source of money but it's unlikely to meet all your needs. The really clever part, perhaps, is to find elsewhere the finance you need to match the strategic vision for your school and the premises. There is another book in this series, *Solutions: Raising Additional Income*, that you may find helpful. In a nutshell, some important additional sources are likely to be

- your school budget

- some categories in the Standards Fund

- major capital bids to the DfES or LEA

- seed challenge funding, which requires the school to provide some new money

- lottery grants

- donations or trust funds (if you're fortunate!)

- your school's foundation, if it has one, such as a church

- fundraising (for example, through a PTA).

4 Managing capital projects efficiently.

You'll need to decide how to manage capital projects in your school. Your LEA is likely to offer a building management service, which your school can buy into. This is often a 'default setting' where you can offload some work and which can provide reassurance.

However, you may prefer the autonomy and flexibility of running things yourself. Maybe your governors have the time and expertise to help. For church schools, your diocese may be able to assist. Or you could employ outside project managers, architects for example, to manage things for you when needed.

> There is much to be said for managing capital projects and their financing directly in school, but do ensure you get good professional advice when you need it. Fees for this can be included in the overall project cost.

Here are three further things to think about when managing capital projects and the associated finance.

Keep the finances together

Exactly as with the Standards Fund (Chapter 5) try to look upon all the sources of funding for capital work in your school as a whole, even though accounting procedures may be separate. It's all part of one big plan for your school.

Organise tendering properly

For works over about £1 000, it's generally necessary to seek tenders or estimates (your school may well choose to do this for some smaller projects). Your LEA will give guidance about this.

When inviting tenders, particularly for substantial projects, it's essential to have a clear specification for the work to give to the firms who wish to tender. You've then made sure that the process is fair and when you receive the tenders you can be confident you are comparing like with like. Make sure that the figures given are quotations and not just estimates.

> A tender specification is a precise technical list of the work you wish to have carried out on a particular job. It needs to be prepared by an appropriate professional, such as an architect, in consultation with you.

SORRY ABOUT THIS. WE HAD A BIT OF TROUBLE WITH THE WINDOWS AND HAD TO ORDER SOME EXTRA LIGHTING.

Of course, this shouldn't preclude you also from having more informal contacts with local firms. Often they can give good advice or ideas about what building solution could be used to solve your problem. This might then be considered in the tender.

Cashflow

Capital projects are by nature expensive. It's always important to check you have sufficient money in your school bank account to cover expenditure you know is coming through. Keep a special check on this when planning the timing and staging of capital projects. Any major building work is liable to unexpected expenses arising during the project. Be prepared for this and build in a contingency.

Voluntary aided (VA) schools – a special case

VA schools have a special legal status. The foundation (usually a church) appoints a majority of the governors, formally employs the staff and owns the school buildings. The foundation determines the character of the school. The *quid pro quo* of these extra freedoms is that the governing body has to provide 10% of most capital costs.

This means that a VA school's devolved capital money is held for you at the DfES. When you wish to use it you need to fill in a form for approval. Once approved, the project can go ahead and you can claim back 90% of the cost from the fund held in your school's name at the DfES.

This can be rather a frustrating bureaucratic process and, as you don't receive the money back until after the job is done, the cashflow can be even more problematic. However, the civil servants who administer the scheme are usually very helpful and can often provide useful advice. It's also reassuring to know that when projects are approved you can be pretty sure they've been managed properly.

In summary

Managing devolved capital funding is an intricate area but with lots of potential to help improve every school. It's important to see premises development as a means to an end – improved teaching and learning – not as something apart.

▶ **Next step**

Consider how your plan for your premises (Asset Management Plan) links to your plan for improving teaching and learning (School Improvement Plan). Are there any areas where the link could be even stronger?

CHAPTER 7

How should the School Fund and other voluntary accounts be managed?

Your school will be raising cash for things like school trips, charities you support, additional equipment or visiting drama groups or entertainers. Usually, such money is managed in a 'Voluntary Fund'.

You may have just one voluntary account, which all 'non-public' money passes through. Many schools, however, have separate voluntary accounts for different purposes. These might include a school journey account, a tuck shop account and a school shop account.

It's up to each school to decide what's best and most straightforward for them. These funds do not contain public money as such but nevertheless it is right, and fair to everyone involved, to manage them as carefully as if they did. This chapter takes a look at what you should do.

You need to

1 ensure all the correct procedures are followed

2 use the money for the purposes you choose

3 make sure good accounts are kept and audited

1 The correct procedures to follow when dealing with voluntary funds.

The school governors, in the end, are responsible for all voluntary funds. However, as head you should ensure the following.

A bank account is opened and ground rules established

Obviously, you'll need a bank account for your voluntary fund. This account should require two signatures on each cheque (from perhaps three or four authorised signatories), so that both people who sign each cheque endorse and validate the purpose of the expenditure. You should be one of the signatories and it's useful to have a fund rule that money won't be spent without your agreement.

Someone is appointed to run the account

The person who manages the fund from day to day could be a secretary or finance officer, a governor, a teacher or someone who holds that role in the school alone. This individual should

- keep day-to-day accounts of all transactions in the fund, according to proper procedures (there are likely to be LEA guidelines about this, even though the money is not theirs)

- bank promptly all money received

- organise payments by the fund

- issue receipts or any other necessary documentation

- reconcile the fund with bank statements

- produce an end of year account (see section 3 on page 38)

Pay by cheque

It's much safer to make payments from the fund by cheque. This means you can check up on any inconsistencies, disputes or problems. Cash payments for services should be avoided.

Avoid using private bank accounts

We don't live in a very trusting world, so never use your own or anyone else's private bank account, however temporarily, to hold money that should be in the school fund. Don't hold on to any cash that belongs to the fund, even for a short time.

> **If you're lucky enough to have a significant balance in your voluntary fund, ensure you keep funds in a deposit account if they are not instantly needed.**

Keep in the black

It's very important to keep watch on the cash flow situation in the voluntary fund. Don't go overdrawn!

Spend the money appropriately

School fund money can be used for many purposes. That's one of its great joys – you can use it to provide some extras that might not be possible or affordable within the main budget. However, it must still be used for the genuine purposes of the school. Sometimes there's a fine distinction. Paying some of the cost of an afternoon tea for a staff member who is leaving may be reasonable. Buying birthday presents for teachers, however nice an idea, would be inappropriate.

2 Using the money for the purposes you want.

The great thing about the school fund is that you don't have to plan for its use in the great detail that is needed for your main budget. There is flexibility and some spontaneity is always possible. However, it's still money for the school and within reason the same principle applies here as we saw in Chapters 5 and 6, that is to use the school voluntary fund to support your school priorities. The school fund is still part of the global pot available to your school, so it's good to use it alongside other monies that you have, in a complementary way.

> It's a good idea to have the purpose of your school fund written down in your school's finance policy. Here's an example to use as a starting point.
>
> *'The School Voluntary Fund exists to provide money to enhance the school and benefit the pupils. Money in the fund is used to support, enrich and add to the provision the school makes.'*

3 It is vital that you produce good accounts and have them audited annually.

Producing accounts

Each year the person running the voluntary fund must produce

- a set of accounts, showing income and expenditure in the previous twelve months

- a statement of cash in hand at the end of the accounting year (also known as a balance sheet).

Neither of these reports needs to be particularly complicated but they must be clear and easy to understand. They can be readily combined into one document. From reading them, people should know unambiguously

- where the money has come from

- what it's been spent on

- how much is left over in the bank accounts.

An example is given opposite.

Notes about the example

1 It's helpful for corresponding items in the receipts and payments column to be shown next to each other so that, for example, people can see that all of the charity collections went in donations and that the tuck shop made a surplus of £109.

2 It's useful to show different headings of expenditure on school equipment (for example music, PE and books) so that people can see in reasonable detail what was purchased. This is helpful as the people seeing the accounts may well have contributed money to the fund and you'll want to show them that the money has been well spent.

3 The bottom two lines of these imaginary accounts are the balance sheet. This shows how the fund's bank balance has been affected by the year's activity. In this case there has been £163 more income (excess of receipts over payments) than expenditure, so naturally the balance has risen by that amount over the year.

PRIMARY SCHOOL VOLUNTARY FUND ACCOUNT
1 SEPTEMBER 2002 to 31 AUGUST 2003

Receipts	£	Payments	£
Charity collections	1287	Charity donations	1287
Contributions from families	960	Gifts and subscriptions	302
Gifts and donations	844	Hospitality	135
Day visits – parent contributions	1763	Day visits – costs	1815
School photograph income	237	Bank charges	10
Book fair	759	Book fair	702
Cycling proficiency fees	156	Cycling proficiency costs	156
Sales (pens, folders, recorders)	368	Purchases for sales	311
Tuck shop income	584	Tuck shop purchases	475
		Books for school	511
		Music equipment	285
		PE equipment	556
		Residential visit subsidy	250
TOTAL RECEIPTS	6958	TOTAL PAYMENTS	6795
Excess Payments		Excess Receipts	163
	6958		**6958**
Excess of Receipts over Payments	163	Excess of Payments over Receipts	0
Balance brought forward	504	Balance carried forward	667

We certify that to the best of our knowledge and belief the accounts shown are correct.

SIGNED by the person who manages the fund and the headteacher.

I have audited the above accounts of the above Fund. In my opinion there has been proper management of the Fund and the above summary of account is a true representation of the Fund's affairs at (date).

SIGNED by the appointed auditor.

This is a simple example of what an audited voluntary fund account, including the balance sheet, might look like.

Audit

Once the accounts have been finalised, they need to go to an auditor. An accountant is often the best person for this, either on a paid or voluntary basis.

However, the work doesn't have to be done by a professional. A governor could work with a teacher, for example, but using a third party ensures financial impartiality and makes it easier to handle any mismanagement that might occur.

The auditors have to check for two things.

• The money has actually been received and spent as the accounts say.

• The money has been spent on the proper purposes of the school voluntary fund.

In summary

Your voluntary fund is a very useful resource for the school. To use it most effectively spend it in conjunction with other school monies, though with flexibility and spontaneity, to achieve your school objectives.

▶ **Next step**

Check that the management and accounting procedures for your voluntary funds are correctly set up and are being followed.

CHAPTER  8

How can I ensure my budget management supports the SIP, targets, and high standards?

This chapter is arguably the most important in the book. We've seen that managing your budget is a precious freedom worth protecting. Therefore we need to be able to account properly for the way we've spent the school's money. We need to do this in a way that

- clearly shows how effective our spending has been
- helps us to evaluate and then plan for the future
- we don't find painful or excessively bureaucratic.

Your School Improvement Plan (SIP) is probably the main tool you use to link money to your strategy for the school. This chapter looks at a simple and successful model of how to do this, which you can readily adapt and use to suit your circumstances and preferences.

You need to

1 decide exactly what you want to achieve for the children

2 decide how you're going to achieve it and what it will cost – then manage the process

3 keep some simple evidence and evaluate how successful you've been

1 The model explained.

The model is very simple and what it contains is unlikely to surprise you. Its simplicity, however, is its virtue.

Particularly intricate, or imposed, forms of development planning in schools can often become counterproductive. Few people fully understand what such plans mean, or see them as being relevant to their day-to-day work.

With this model, the important thing is just to focus on what matters and nothing else.

> **This chapter helps make the link between financial management and school improvement.**

Here's the model.

Step 1

Decide on, and define very precisely, something that you want to achieve in the school.

Step 2

Work out how you will best achieve this, and how much it's all going to cost.

Step 3

Put your costed plan of action into practice and monitor what happens. Keep some simple but reliable evidence of what's been achieved.

Step 4

Evaluate how effective your expenditure has been by comparing what has happened with what you wanted in Step 1.

Step 5

Start again!

2 Decide exactly what you want to achieve for the children – set your own targets.

Every year when you work out your SIP, you almost certainly have some kind of consultation or other mechanism for deciding what the priorities are going to be. This probably involves governors and staff and maybe pupils, parents and others. At this stage, using the model suggested here, it's really important to be

- very precise and focused when discussing and then putting into words the priorities you choose

- firmly focused on what your school exists for – children's learning and achievement.

> This book is not about target-setting. However, to manage your finances most successfully you must know very precisely and unambiguously what spending the money in the way you've chosen is supposed to achieve. That's where targets – which you have chosen – can be useful.

From your priorities should come some desired outcomes or targets. These will be about improving the school in some way, or raising standards even further. Here are a few example targets that are clearly focused on the pupils and their learning and achievement.

Example target

1 In a representative sample of work in all subjects, Y2 children spell 95% of high frequency words correctly.

2 All children identify five key questions at the start of all history and geography topics and, at the end of the topic, evaluate how well they have answered these questions using our school criteria.

3 Every child in KS2 chooses to join an extra-curricular sporting club.

Targets like this are much more useful than 'improving spelling in context', 'giving children opportunities to undertake enquiry work' or 'increasing the number of children joining sports clubs' because everyone will know exactly what the school is trying to achieve with the children.

At this stage you may well group targets in particular areas. For instance, if raising standards in spelling was a key strategic aim of your school, the first example above could be one of a set of targets within that overall goal.

The target examples given above are all to do with pupil learning and achievement in one way or another. This is appropriate because that's your school's business. But there's no need to go to extremes. If part of your SIP is to provide new furniture or redecorate the hall it's pointless to try to contrive targets relating to pupil outcomes unless the link is absolutely clear-cut.

Don't set too many targets either. This will only become overwhelming. Just pick out a few key areas which are most important to your school.

> At the target-setting stage, don't even think about how you're going to achieve them. Just focus on where you want to get to. When you're quite sure about this, move on to the next stage.

3 Next, decide how you're going to achieve your targets and how much money you're going to spend – work out your strategies.

The best teaching is characterised by not confusing learning objectives with activities. The same principle applies here. Once you've determined *what* you want to achieve, then and only then is the time to work out *how* you're going to do it. This means working out the strategies that are going to enable your targets to be reached.

The strategies you choose might well include a mixture of

• opportunities for staff training

• buying some new equipment

• using the services of an expert consultant

• organising a different pattern of staffing – such as some additional teaching assistant hours

• giving teachers opportunities to team teach, or to work alongside each other

• giving subject leaders or senior staff time to monitor what's happening.

All these are likely to involve spending money, so you need to cost out accurately each strategy you choose. These costs will then need to be built into your school budget. When you do this, you're linking your improvement planning process to your budget-setting process in a very direct and effective way. You're linking it all to clear intended pupil outcomes. For more detail about linking your school improvement planning to your budget-setting see Chapter 11 of *Solutions: Setting Your Budget*.

Having got this part right, you're then able to manage your finances most efficiently. You need to ensure that as the year progresses you spend the money allocated to the strategies you've decided upon.

4 Keep some brief, valid evidence. Using this, check out and evaluate how successful you've been in achieving your original targets.

When you get to the point where you've carried out all your strategies, and paid for them, you need to work out the extent to which you've achieved your original targets. You need to have decided what evidence is necessary to work out how well you've done.

> Don't allow yourself to get bogged down in keeping reams of evidence. This is your process. Keep it simple and manageable.

You don't need masses of evidence. Let's look again at our three example targets from Section 1, but this time with the evidence needed for each one.

Once you've got your evidence, a simple evaluation needs to be made of what's happened. This could be done in your senior management team.

You'll need to consider the following.

• Did we reach our target? Did we miss it? Did we exceed it?

• Whichever way things turned out, what factors were at work?

• Where do we need to go next? Have we finished with this aspect? Can we move it onto the backburner? Does it need more focused attention?

Example target	Evidence needed
1 In a representative sample of work in all subjects, Y2 children spell 95% of high frequency words correctly.	The percentage of key words spelled correctly in the sample, with annotated photocopies of some of the sample.
2 All children identify five key questions at the start of all history and geography topics and, at the end of the topic, evaluate how well they have answered these questions using our school criteria.	A record of the check made of how well the children's work complied with the target, with photocopied examples of a small sample of the children's questions and evaluations.
3 Every child in KS2 chooses to join an extra-curricular sporting club.	Membership lists or registers of the sporting clubs in the school.

- How cost-effective has this been? How good a use of our money has it turned out to be?

You'd be much less able to make that final judgement about the use and management of finance without the original targets. This evaluation will, of course, help you in deciding your priorities, targets and spending plans for the next cycle.

It's a good idea to keep all the work you do, from the initial target-setting to your evidence and evaluation, in one place – say your SIP file. From this you'll be clear what the whole process achieved for the children and whether you spent and managed your school's money effectively. Importantly, you'll also be able to demonstrate this clearly to anyone else.

In summary

Thankfully, financial management is not only about good accounting procedures and keeping an eye on the bottom line. It's about choosing and achieving good clear outcomes for children. You can do this by setting out your strategic aims, linking your budget firmly to crystal-clear targets, and ensuring your expenditure matches your plans. Then you keep some evidence of what is achieved as a result.

▶ Next step

Now have a look at the way you put together your SIP or do whole-school target-setting. Could you include, adapt or develop the use of the model in this chapter? If so, do it in the style and format that suits your school best.

CHAPTER 9

What needs to happen with in-year monitoring?

This chapter looks at the down-to-earth business of monitoring your school's expenditure during the financial year. This means making sure everything is going to plan or is at least under control.

You almost certainly won't be doing everything yourself. As we saw in Chapter 3, your finance officer can take much of the work off your shoulders. Your governors have an important role too. But you will be the one who makes sure everything happens effectively.

You'll need to monitor your school's budget position regularly. Many heads do it monthly but the choice is yours. You'll also need to report to governors periodically. This chapter takes you through the monitoring process, starting from the point when you pick up the printout or spreadsheet showing your school's spending in the financial year so far.

You need to

1 check your staffing costs

2 monitor all other aspects of the budget

3 check the bottom line and make an overall year-end forecast

4 ensure your budget reports are right for their purpose and audience

5 check your cashflow situation

6 deal with any issues that have become apparent

1 The first priority is to check your staffing expenditure.

Many primary schools spend about 80% of their budget on salaries and associated costs, so any slip-ups or unforeseen changes here can be very significant. Above all else, staffing budgets need to be managed with care.

> Using percentages in budget monitoring is not essential but it does help to make large financial figures easier to understand at a glance.

Extrapolate using percentages

Extrapolating using percentages is probably the most effective way of checking your staffing expenditure.

This means that you should set up your financial printout so that it shows expenditure not only in cash terms but also as a percentage of the budget originally set.

You then extrapolate from this what percentage of the original budget you think you will have spent by the financial year-end. This can then be expressed as a cash sum.

An example of the extrapolation process using percentages

Below is a possible line on a budget printout for teaching staff for the end of September (six months into the financial year).

You would expect that at this time of year about 50% of this budget would have been spent because teachers are generally paid in regular monthly instalments. In our example it's looking good at 49.66%. In other months, of course, the expected percentages will be different (naturally, all things being equal, you are likely to spend about one-twelfth or 8.33% of the budget each month).

You should use the information that you have to forecast what you think will have been spent at year-end. Then in the variance column you enter the difference between your original budget and your forecast. In the example above things look pretty much on target. But whether or not things are as you expect, making this year-end forecast is a most important part of your

Budget heading	Original budget set (£)	Expenditure to date (£)	Percentage spent	Year-end forecast	Variance
E01 Teaching Staff	253000	125631	49.66		

Figure 1

monitoring and will need to take into account any possible changes.

For instance, in the September example shown, new teachers may have started work in your school, while others have left. Also, many teachers may have received increments, though these should have been included in the original budget figure.

Overall, these changes may either save the school money or cost more than the original budget figure, depending on the salary points of all the teachers concerned. Whatever the circumstances, you need to take account of the expected variations in your year-end forecast.

If you find that there is a difference between your expenditure to date and what you had expected, you need to decide whether this is a *material discrepancy*. If the difference is more than about 1% it is likely to be

material and you should check carefully what has caused it. Could it be

• an arithmetical error?

• an unforeseen change in costs which needs to be dealt with?

• a mistake by your payroll provider, or a clerical error within the school?

Then repeat this process for all the staffing budget headings

Having done this for the teachers' budget heading, you need to repeat the process for each of your staffing budget headings. Adding all of these up – which your software will probably do automatically – will give you your total expenditure and year-end forecast for staffing as a whole. This will come in useful later (see pages 51 and 53).

Below is our September example again. This time the table shows how things look after

Budget Heading/ CFR Account Code	Original budget set (£)	Expenditure to date (£)	Percentage spent	Year-end forecast (£)	Variance (£)
E01 Teaching Staff	253000	125631	49.66	252500	500
E02 Supply Staff	5000	3214	64.28	6400	+1400
E03 Education Support Staff	28450	13872	48.76	28450	0
E04 Premises Staff	22800	12386	54.32	23500	+700
E05 Admin & Clerical Staff	23500	12987	55.26	25200	+1700
E06 Catering Staff	0	0	0	0	0
E07 Costs of other staff	3230	1510	46.75	3230	0
Total Staffing	**335980**	**169600**	**50.48**	**339280**	**+3300**

Figure 2

49

the extrapolation process has been done for all the staffing headings. Remember, this example is halfway through the financial year. The headings shown are those used for staffing under Consistent Financial Reporting (CFR). They are known as Account Codes.

In this case, an overall staffing overspend of £3 300 is expected at year-end. It may be possible to assimilate this or some remedial action may be needed. This is covered in Section 6. However, before getting that far we need to look at non-staffing costs.

> ### Check your payroll statement every month
>
> It's sensible to check carefully for accuracy the monthly statement that your payroll provider sends you showing how much your school has been charged for each staff member. Make sure that people have been paid from the correct account code. You then know that the overall budget figures you're working with are correct.

2 Then monitor all other (non-staffing) parts of the budget.

You can now carry out a similar extrapolation process for all other aspects of the budget – equipment, supplies, utility costs, etc. There are some differences between these and staffing account codes.

■ Difference 1

The sums of money are usually much smaller. Hence any discrepancies, although they should be considered, are much less likely to be material.

■ Difference 2

For many areas of non-staffing expenditure, spending may well be less evenly spread. For example, heating costs will be at their highest in the winter. Basic stock such as paper, pencils and exercise books may be purchased in a block in late summer for the start of the school year. This means that percentage extrapolations are often much less helpful.

■ Difference 3

Management of many non-staff budgets may be delegated to other members of staff (see Chapter 4). Therefore, tight central control is not helpful as long as the budgets are not being overspent. Again this means that for monitoring purposes the rate of spending may be variable over the year.

Each time you monitor the budget you'll still need to check all areas of non-staffing expenditure, look for any discrepancies, and make a realistic year-end forecast. But you may well find that the process can and should be a little more flexible than when you're monitoring staffing costs.

> It can be useful to check that your hardworking staff, who have been delegated responsibility for parts of the budget, don't leave spending so late that there is an unseemly rush close to the financial year-end!

3 When you've monitored each budget heading, look at the bottom line and make an overall year-end forecast.

Your financial printout or spreadsheet will probably give you a bottom line figure for all expenditure so far. You'll also have made your year-end forecasts. If you add all these forecasts together you'll have an overall prediction of your total spending in the financial year. The variance column will show how much this either exceeds or comes under the original budget set. In turn, this information may prompt you to take action (see page 53).

> If it is possible that the LEA may alter your school budget during the financial year, because of a change in pupil numbers for example, try to take this into account as best you can alongside your year-end forecast.

4 Ensure your budget reports are fit for the audience and purpose.

So far we've looked at budget monitoring that you do personally. But you'll also need to share monitoring information with others. The amount of detail that you need may not always be appropriate or helpful for other groups. Here are the most important examples.

Governors

You'll need to present monitoring figures to your governing body's finance committee or equivalent as needed. They should see the bottom line figures for expenditure, year-end forecast and variance, but the overall level of detail they need depends on what arrangement you have with them.

Governors are unlikely to need to see a detailed breakdown of all the curriculum subject budgets, for example. CFR Account Code E19 (Learning Resources) should suffice. An overall energy figure (CFR Account Code E16), rather than one which is separated out into oil, gas and electricity, is likely to be adequate for their purposes.

Your finance software may be able to run off tailor-made reports for you.

Staff

Members of staff with particular budget responsibilities will need to have access to detailed breakdowns of their areas. You may well want to share the broader budget situation with senior staff especially, so that they can be involved in thinking through and understanding the issues. Again, the detail you need may not be necessary for them. Alternatively you may only need to show part of the budget – say that for curriculum equipment – for staff discussions concerning that area.

LEA

Your LEA will require monitoring returns from you in a format they choose. If you're doing the extrapolation process on a regular basis, you should have all the information you need for this. The LEA needs information so it can

- account for the overall expenditure on education

- have an overview of how money is being spent in schools.

Unless your school is in deficit or has significant management problems, your LEA should not require too many financial returns from you – quarterly or half-yearly returns should normally be enough. Nor, of course, should the LEA ever seek to tell you how to spend your delegated budget, even as 'advice'.

5 Check your cashflow situation.

Cashflow involves making sure you have enough money in your bank account at any time to cover all the money you're going to need to pay out. This is unlikely to be problematic for you unless

• you're in deficit

• you have very small reserves, or none

• you have very significant sums of money to pay out all at the same time.

If you're in any of these situations you may have to ensure that you plan carefully to spread expenditure out across the year to ensure you always have sufficient funds available.

6 Deal with whatever financial issues your monitoring makes apparent.

Having been through your regular monitoring process as outlined and come up with the bottom line figures for expenditure, year-end forecast and variance, you and your governors need to decide what to do as a result of this information.

In broad terms, there are three possible scenarios to consider.

1 Your overall year-end forecast indicates a budget overspend

This is the most difficult position to be in. However, if your monitoring is accurate, at least you have some time to deal with it. Essentially you have three options, which can be combined with each other.

• Reduce your spending in some way, for instance by not making a planned purchase, or by reducing staff hours (where you have flexibility).

• Use any reserves you have to cover the overspend.

• Raise money from a source other than your school budget, for example by fundraising.

Whichever option or combination of options you choose, always try to minimise the effect on your main school priorities, especially those relating to children's learning.

2 Your overall year-end forecast indicates a budget underspend

In this situation, enjoy yourself! You have some positive options which again can be combined.

- Save the money up for a larger project by adding it to your reserves.

- Bring forward any important projects you have planned and do them earlier than you expected would be possible.

- Add the money as additional funding to a project you're already undertaking and give yourself the opportunity to do it even better.

3 Your overall year-end forecast indicates that your budget is on course to break even

In this case, you need do nothing except continue to monitor. Well done for having budgeted so accurately in the first place! If, however, your overall balanced budget position is covering a situation where some budget headings are considerably overspending and being balanced by others which are underspending, you should consider using virements. This is covered in Chapter 10.

In summary

You need to monitor your budget regularly to keep on top of it, and then take any necessary action according to your school priorities. The end of September check is possibly the most useful. This is because it's exactly halfway through the financial year and any autumn staff changes, which you may not have known about when you set the budget, have taken place. So you have plenty of accurate information to go on and there's still ample time left to deal with any issues.

▶ Next step

Make sure you have a table for budget monitoring, with columns for percentage spending, year-end forecast and variance for each budget heading (account code). Your financial software may do this, but if not it's a good idea to make a spreadsheet, as this can do the sums for you.

CHAPTER 10 How do virements work?

Sometimes you will find yourself wanting to move money from one budget heading to another. This could be because an unforeseen event or change in circumstances necessitates a change of plans. Alternatively, it could be that when monitoring your budget you predict that an account code is going to underspend and so you want to use the money you've saved somewhere else.

When you move money like this, from one budget heading, or account code, to another during the financial year, it's called viring.

As headteacher, you normally have some freedom to make virements but there are usually limits to what you can do without involving the governing body in the decision.

This chapter outlines how virements work and shows how they can help you manage your school's finances.

You need to

1 have a policy decision about who can make virements

2 make the virements when needed

3 keep a careful record of all virements

1 Decide, as a matter of policy, who can make virements.

As the day-to-day manager of the school's budget you'll need to have scope to make virements. It's unlikely that anyone else on the staff will need to do so. It may be, however, that the governing body, in its strategic role, will want to be involved when larger virements are under consideration.

Therefore, it's necessary to have a school policy which allows the head to make virements up to a certain amount – say £1 000 or £2 000. Virements above this would need your finance committee's approval.

Make sure that this is written explicitly in your finance policy.

2 Make the virements when needed.

The circumstances when virements are needed include

• a necessary change in priorities which has taken place since the budget was originally set

• an unforeseen event which costs or saves money

• an indication from budget monitoring that an account code is going to overspend and the money to pay for this needs to come from somewhere

• an indication from budget monitoring that an account code is going to underspend and the money can be used elsewhere.

> Some virements may be made within account codes. For example, moving £200 from your geography budget into history is all within the account code E19 Learning Resources. This may mean that you don't consider it a formal virement at all but just a transfer within a code.

Case study 1

The winter is particularly mild and by February it is clear that the energy budget is very healthy. Additionally, astute purchasing in bulk has reduced the costs of exercise books and other basic equipment. The school has a plan to install a computer workstation in its library but it was not possible to budget for it to go ahead this year. By viring £700 from E16 Energy and £300 from E19 Learning Resources into E20 ICT Learning Resources, it is possible to spend the £1000 to purchase the computer workstation early.

Case study 2

A group of children in Year 2 is really struggling with their writing. As a result, the leadership team has decided that it would be sensible to set up a regular booster group for these pupils, using a supply teacher, at a cost of £650. To cover this cost, the sum of £650 is vired from E12 Building Maintenance and Improvement to E02 Supply Staff. This means that the hall cannot be decorated until next year, which is a great shame but everyone agrees that this is a sensible change in priorities.

Case study 3

A new teacher, who is on a much higher scale than the person he replaces, has been appointed from January. This is going to cost the school £2 700 in this financial year and so account code E01 Teaching Staff is going to overspend by that amount. The head and governors look at ways of covering this figure and decide that only £1 000 can come from their reserves. The hard decision has to be taken, therefore, to reduce release time for senior staff in the spring term to cover the cost. A virement of £1 700 is made from E02 Supply Staff to E01 Teaching Staff.

3 Keep a careful record of all virements.

It's important to record all virements, and the reasons for making them. This can be used for governors and also if you are audited. It's a good idea to keep a virements book for this purpose.

Your finance computer software may have a column called 'Revised Budget' or similar, which can confirm, for any account code, any changes caused by virements during the financial year. It's important that all virements are shown on your finance computer system.

In summary

Virements are a useful management tool for keeping things tidy and clear when you need to make financial changes.

▶ Next step

Virements can often be used very effectively to bring forward expenditure which you thought would have to wait until another year. Why not see if the outcomes of your budget monitoring (Chapter 9) are giving you opportunities to do this?

CHAPTER 11

What day-to-day financial routines need to happen?

Throughout the book we have looked at how to manage finances using the information you have in front of you. To be able to do this there are certain day-to-day routines you need to use to keep the accounts accurate, up to date and secure.

As head you're unlikely to be doing these things yourself much of the time – they normally fall within the role of a finance officer, as we saw in Chapter 3. However, you'll need to make sure that the right procedures are in place and that they're being carried out effectively. This chapter provides a checklist of what needs to be done.

You need to

1 ensure all day-to-day routines are organised

2 make sure procedures which occur on a regular, timed basis are in place

3 take care that financial information, as well as cash, is kept secure

1 Ensuring all day-to-day routines are organised.

It's important to be sure that basic routines are well established, as money comes into and out of your school bank account daily. Here's a checklist of the main procedures you'll need.

- Raising orders using your school's system and then manually posting or faxing these orders to the suppliers.

- Scrutinising all invoices for irregularities – for example, checking that the school has actually received the goods/service concerned or that the VAT charged is correct.

- Preparing school cheques and arranging for the authorised people to sign them.

- Sending out cheques, with the correct information for the recipients as to what they are for, including any reference numbers.

- Printing off individual budget heading reports for budget holders to enable them to monitor and plan their expenditure.

- Running overall budget monitoring reports for the head and governors, in the format which it has been agreed will be most useful (see Chapter 9).

- Paying cash and cheques into the school's bank accounts.

- Dealing with others who may send money to the school – for example, the PTA treasurer.

- Running the school fund and any other voluntary accounts accurately (see Chapter 7).

> **Chapter 4 gives a procedure for ordering resources and paying invoices that ensures honesty and checks and balances. You might want to refer to it at this point.**

2 Making sure that procedures which occur regularly are in place.

Other procedures occur on a regular basis at particular times – every term or month for example. These are likely to include

* sending VAT returns to the LEA so that tax you have paid can be refunded – schools are not normally required to pay VAT

* checking monthly school budget and Standards Fund advances from the LEA, and then putting these on your school's accounting system

* ensuring that any direct debits – the main one of which is probably staff salaries – are accounted for and checked

* checking your payroll provider's listing of salaries paid to employees and supply staff to ensure it is correct, and then following up any queries and errors (see Chapter 9)

* reconciling the school's bank statement against payments and income

* reconciliation of all expenditure and income, including petty cash

* drafting any routine financial returns to the LEA (see Chapter 9).

3 Keeping financial information and records, as well as cash, secure.

Financial information on the school may well be sensitive or confidential. It's also necessary to guard against theft. So you need to make sure that reasonable security measures are in place.

All members of staff or governors who have access to budget information or cash need to make sure that

* any items such as chequebooks and petty cash that could be misused or stolen are kept securely locked up, preferably in a safe

- all personal records, such as pay details, are kept secure and never left lying around or visible on an unattended computer screen

- sensitive or personal information is not disclosed to those who have no need or right to know it

- financial records held on computer can only be accessed by those with a need to know, using a password system

- all information kept on a hard disk or network is frequently backed up.

Schools are often very open places, both physically and in terms of the ready availability of information. In this trusting and open culture we have to be doubly sure that sensitive information and valuable items are well protected.

In summary

This book has lots of ideas and solutions for good financial management. To use them effectively, basic day-to-day routines need to be well established. These enable you to run your budget efficiently and proactively.

▶ **Next step**

Use this chapter to check that you've got the right systems in place and that those who are running them know what's expected. You may also want to get yourself geared up for audit – see Chapter 15.

CHAPTER

What needs to be sorted out at the end of the financial year?

On 1 April a new financial year begins and the old one ends. This is the time when we have to take stock of what has happened in the preceding year and make sure we're organised for the next. Fortunately, sorting all this out can usually be done over a period of a few weeks, even months, during the spring. It doesn't really happen overnight!

Nevertheless, it's a busy time and we have to get it right. This chapter will help guide you through.

You need to

1 for the year-end, organise your financial information in good time, make a final balance of all expenditure and income, then report on this

2 for the new financial year, do the calculations, set up your new budget and tell your colleagues what they have to spend

1 Get your financial data up to date and organised, get a final balance of all income and expenditure at the year-end and report on this.

In January or February it's a good idea to plan ahead with your finance officer to get the following tasks done.

Get the accounts up to date

Your bursar or finance officer will have been keeping the accounts up to date throughout the year. As you approach year-end, it's time to check that everything that should have gone through the school accounts has done so. Ideally, you don't want to be carrying any debts into the new financial year and you should make sure that if anyone owes the school money it is paid up before 31 March. During March it's sensible to be chasing this.

> It makes sense to create a deadline for budget holders to place orders well before the end of the financial year. The beginning of February is a reasonable time. This means that there is time for the whole process of ordering, paying and accounting (Chapter 4) to go through before the year-end.

Organise any debtors and creditors

Life is not always straightforward. If, come 31 March, you are owed money or owe someone else, this needs to be set up on your finance system as 'debtors and creditors'. When this is done, you'll be able to see

- what amounts are still due to go through the books

- how these debtor and creditor figures fit into the final accounts.

> Debtors and creditors always muddy the waters a bit. It's worth planning ahead to avoid them if you can.

Tie up the Standards Fund and devolved capital money

As we saw in Chapters 5 and 6, these two parts of your funding are accounted for separately. You'll need to ensure there are complete year-end financial statements for them. Again, your school's finance system should be able to do this for you as long as everything is up to date.

Remember that at some point you lose any unspent money under these headings. For the Standards Fund this is now usually at the end of August. For capital money, it's after three years. Therefore, it's well worth ensuring at year-end that where possible you have categorised appropriate spending under the Standards Fund or capital headings rather than under your main delegated budget, which you won't lose.

Get your balance, and work out your rollover

Once you (or more likely your finance officer) have done all this, your computer system should be able to print off

- the total income received under each heading

- the final spending under each account code

- the overall total balance of income and expenditure for the year

- how much is left unspent – your rollover.

> In-year monitoring (Chapter 9) will have told you what to expect in the final balance but even so it can be an interesting and possibly salutary task to check the final figures against your original budget.

Report to the LEA and to the school community

This final information needs to be reported to various audiences.

- *You, the head*, need very detailed information under CFR codes and the sub-headings you've set up, to help you plan next year's budget.

- *Your relevant governors' committee* should see a basic run-off of the final accounts under the CFR codes or in whatever format you have agreed with them.

- *Your LEA* will need your final figures so that it can include them within the authority's overall accounts.

- *Parents* – at this time it can be helpful to put together a straightforward table ready to include in the next governors' annual report to parents. It's generally best to keep this simple by amalgamating account codes together under broad headings.

This table gives an example of how you could show the school's financial position in the governors' annual report to parents.

Heading	Original budget set (£)	Actual expenditure (£)
Staffing	401000	399552
Premises	36627	34305
Equipment	32720	33372
Supplies and Services	14695	12893
Total Expenditure	**485042**	**480122**
Other Income		(32291)
Net Expenditure		**447831**
Formula Budget		(453296)
Unspent this year		5465
Unspent from previous year		14297
Unspent carried into next year		19762

Figure 3

2 For the new financial year do the calculations, set up your budget and let people know what they can spend.

While all the work is going on to close down the old year, you'll also be aiming to have your new budget set up as soon as possible. Setting the budget is the subject of another book in this series *Solutions: Your Budget*. However, some ideas about the principles involved in this are given in Chapter 8.

Two important management tasks follow on directly after you've set your budget for the new year.

- Ensure that the new budget is quickly entered on your school finance system, under each account centre or heading, and that any information the LEA requires concerning the new budget is passed on to them.

- Tell budget holders what money is available to them to spend and, if appropriate, what the agreed desired outcomes of the spending are (see Chapter 4).

In summary

There's a lot to sort out as one financial year gives way to another. However, it doesn't all have to be done at once. Planning ahead, and a systematic approach, will see you through.

▶ **Next step**

You have detailed information about where your school's money has been spent. It can be useful to compare this with what other schools have been doing. We look at this subject next, in Chapter 13.

CHAPTER 13

How can I compare my school's budget with others?

The process of comparing the way one school uses its budget with another is usually known as *financial benchmarking*. This can be a worthwhile thing to do. It means that you'll be able to see

* the broad financial priorities of other schools

* whether there are any useful lessons you can learn from the way other schools use their budgets.

This is all becoming much easier under Consistent Financial Reporting (CFR) because all schools are using the same account codes or budget headings. You can now be reasonably sure you're comparing like with like.

The government has brought in CFR because it gives a national structure and makes accountability, aggregating and comparison easier. However, whilst CFR's increased transparency has many advantages, it's also clear that it could be used to try to tell schools what proportion of budgets ought to be spent on each area. This could diminish the precious freedom that the law gives us. So we need to remember that financial benchmarking doesn't mean we should feel pressurised to match any model or all fall into line with each other. *Vive la difference!* – as long as we know why.

You need to

1 find the right data from other schools to compare

2 ask yourself the right questions about the data

1 Finding the right data from other schools to compare.

There are various ways of getting the data you need, with different pros and cons. Here are some ideas.

> Because school budgets vary considerably in size, it's obviously much easier to benchmark using percentages, rather than actual cash sums. But remember that economies of scale in larger schools may mean that their staffing budgets, as a percentage of the whole, are lower than those in smaller schools.

> You may find that LEAs hold overall comparative information about the spending of their schools in specific areas – special educational needs is a common example. It may be possible to use these figures for benchmarking in these particular aspects.

> Some LEAs provide their schools with such data so that they can compare their spending patterns with schools of a similar type and size.

Idea 1

Get together with a local group of heads – or even just one other head – and agree to benchmark your budgets jointly.

If you do this, make sure you agree ground rules beforehand and establish trust. The aim of the session should be to compare budgets and discuss the differences so that you can share ideas and learn from each other.

Pros

- You can ask each other direct questions and deal with any queries.

- If you're working in the same area your school circumstances may be similar.

- You can follow up any developments readily.

- You may know, or be able to discuss, how effective each school has been in using money to achieve particular outcomes.

Cons

- If you're within the same LEA, there may not be a great breadth of practice.

- The discussion could become too cosy if you're not careful.

- If a school is clearly having a problem it could be uncomfortable.

Idea 2

Visit the Audit Commission's website, www.schools.audit-commission.gov.uk, and use the benchmarking tool there.

The site allows you to compare the way you spend your budget with a database of 'similar' schools.

Pros

• You are comparing information with many other schools.

• You do this by yourself, so there's no possibility of awkwardness.

• The site helps you to interpret the data you find.

• It's easy to be rigorous and ask searching questions of yourself.

Cons

• This is not a personal process and there's no one else to learn from.

• You can't ask questions.

• It can be quite time-consuming.

• You won't know the pupil outcomes that have resulted from the spending patterns you can see.

Idea 3

Get information from schools that are further afield and analyse it.

You could get in touch with schools, perhaps in other LEAs, that you have contact with, or use contacts within your LEA. Ask if you can see or exchange budget information.

Pros

• The information you have is from a wide area.

• You may be able to contact the heads of the schools involved for information.

• It may be easier to be rigorous than when using very local schools.

Cons

• The information you have may not be complete.

• Other schools may feel you are prying.

• It could be a lengthy task to set this up.

• You may not know the circumstances of the other schools very well.

2 Asking the right questions.

Once you have the data for benchmarking you need to interpret it and ask the right questions about it.

- What are the main differences/similarities in these schools' use of their money?

- Why are these schools' spending patterns so similar/different?

- Has another school found an innovative approach to using money effectively that I could use or adapt?

- Are any schools obviously achieving particularly good outcomes for their children in a cost-effective way?

- Can I learn anything from other schools about how I could allocate my school's budget even more efficiently?

- Are there any inventive ways of reducing administration and support costs to put more money into the curriculum? (CFR makes a clear distinction between these two types of expenditure.)

In summary

Comparing budgets with other schools – financial benchmarking – can be a useful process if it's done well. It may enable you to learn from and share with others, and find ways of spending your school budget even more effectively.

▶ **Next step**

Financial benchmarking can go very well with Best Value, which prompts us to ask searching but positive questions about our schools. This is covered next, in Chapter 14.

CHAPTER 14

What should I do about value for money, Best Value and Ofsted?

Terms like 'value for money' and 'Best Value' can sound so off-putting, even ominous at times. Isn't the value of our work in schools obvious, we might ask?

However, looked at positively, value for money and Best Value can be quite useful management tools. This is because they are only about money in so far as our management of it impacts on outcomes for children. If we think these terms through for ourselves then any future Ofsted judgement about them need not unduly worry us. More importantly, it can help us improve our schools. This chapter explains how.

You need to

1 understand what value for money means for schools and how Ofsted measures it

2 know and apply the four principles of Best Value

1 Understanding the concept of value for money in schools and how Ofsted measures this.

Value for money in a school is simply explained by the following equation.

$$\frac{\text{The school's effectiveness}}{\text{The cost of running the school}} \quad (= \text{Value for Money})$$

In other words if the school is effective, has low costs and the budget is efficiently managed, it will be providing good or very good value for money. However, if the school is effective but has a larger than average budget to spend the value for money it provides will be lower.

So it's no bad thing to ask yourself some robust questions about the cost-effectiveness of your school. Does your school provide good value for money overall? Could more be done for children with the money available? This will take you on from the financial benchmarking strategy outlined in Chapter 13.

When you're thinking about how effective your school is, consider candidly how good the following are.

• Educational standards in relation to the ability and prior attainment of the pupils.

• The quality of teaching.

• The breadth and interest of the curriculum.

• The provision of extra-curricular activities.

• The attitudes and values children gain from the school.

> The better the self-evaluation procedures your school has, the better you'll be able to judge value for money.

When you ask yourself these questions and then relate them to your budget you'll be following exactly the same process that Ofsted inspectors do when making their judgement about value for money. There isn't any magic formula involved. Inspectors will judge the effectiveness of your school against what they consider should be achievable with the money available. It's best to pre-empt them.

> It's hard to judge value for money without making comparisons with other schools. You need some points of reference. See Chapter 13 for ideas about getting together with other schools for benchmarking.

> Following the targeted planning and evaluation process outlined in Chapter 8 helps to achieve and assess good value for money.

2 Knowing and applying the four principles of Best Value.

Best Value is a government strategy that aims to enable public services to improve continually. It is concerned with value for money but goes further. It can sound disconcerting but actually it's based on good management principles and its clear structure can help us. It applies legally to local authorities but not to schools. However, we are asked to follow the principles of Best Value, and Ofsted evaluates how well this is done in every inspection.

> When you think about Best Value it's sensible to do so with your governors and senior staff.

In this section, we'll look at the four Best Value principles and some questions that you might want to think about in respect of each. Then there are references to two publications and four websites which you could use to take your thinking further.

The four Best Value principles – the four Cs

1 Challenge

This is all about deciding whether the services you're currently providing are the right ones to suit current and future circumstances.

Ask yourself
• Why are we providing this particular service/curriculum activity in this way? Do we still need it?

• Are there other things our community now needs us to accomplish or make available in the school?

• Are there better ways of doing some of the things we're doing?

2 Compare

Here the issue is comparing what we're doing with others and using this information to help us decide whether and how we can improve. The direct contacts we have with other schools can of course be very helpful here. Ofsted PANDA reports also provide useful information, as can financial benchmarking (see Chapter 13).

Ask yourself
• When we compare ourselves with others, especially schools with similar circumstances to ours, what are we clearly doing very well? What can we improve?

- Are we consistently successful in all parts of the school?

- What do we need to do to maintain, or reach, the standards achieved by the most effective schools?

3 Consult

In this area we're trying to keep in close touch with the needs and wants of the community we serve, and respond to them. Consulting people can provide good ideas and gain their commitment to improvement projects.

Ask yourself

- Which groups within the school community is it helpful to consult over any given change or improvement project?

- How can we find out what people think of the service we're providing?

4 Compete

This final principle deals with getting things done at the right price. It's partly about the value for money the school is providing and partly about getting good terms when buying services from outside the school.

Ask yourself

- Could we provide this service as effectively but more cheaply?

- Do we have good arrangements for tendering and getting the most economic goods and services from our suppliers? (This doesn't always mean accepting the cheapest quote).

- Are our financial procedures working well?

In the references section on Page 79 you'll find some useful, authoritative resources that might help you answer the challenging Best Value questions for your school. Also, by using the ideas in the chapters of this book, you'll be applying Best Value principles.

In summary

Thinking about value for money and Best Value can be demanding and perhaps cause apprehension. But if we use the processes outlined in this chapter it can also be stimulating and productive, helping us to improve our schools.

▶ Next step

Have a go at making the link between your school's income and its overall effectiveness. Why not use the Best Value model – it can be helpful. Keep it in perspective and use the guidance to focus and support the self-evaluation already going on in your school.

CHAPTER 15

How can I deal with an audit?

If the LEA audits your school, essentially two things will be looked at.

- Is the school's money being spent with probity – ie. honestly?
- Is the school's money being spent for appropriate purposes, with systems in place to ensure this?

Auditors, however sympathetic, are accountants of one sort or another, not educationalists. This means that there is potential for conflict between their values and ours. We are concerned with children and learning. Their main function is to check compliance with a set of rules.

> If your school has a full audit it is likely that all the different aspects will be looked at. Partial audits, with a more limited focus, can be quite common in some LEAs. In either case your LEA should make it clear well in advance what information and records the auditors will need to see.

You could be running the country's most effective school and still fall foul of audit because of a technicality, an oversight or an additional system that needs to be in place. The trouble is that if auditors do consider there to be shortcomings, however minor, in your procedures it can take time and energy to sort them out. This in turn takes you away from what really matters in your school – teaching and learning.

Therefore, it's best to get it as right as you can first time. This chapter aims to help with this by providing two checklists covering the two audit areas above.

You need to

1 take care that your school's procedures ensure honesty

2 make sure your school routines and systems are satisfactory for audit purposes

1 A checklist for ensuring financial honesty in your school.

■ Make certain that policy and practice in your school ensure that everyone who has access to school finances – including voluntary funds – knows that they must be spent on the 'purposes of the school' and understands what this means (Chapters 1 and 7).

■ Don't use the school budget to purchase items for the private use of staff, even if the person concerned fully repays the school.

■ Follow any special financial regulations your LEA imposes (Chapter 1).

■ Give everyone clear roles in financial management (Chapter 3).

■ Make sure that there is always a double-check on all financial transactions – protect everyone by ensuring that money cannot go out of the school without at least two people being involved.

■ Follow a clear procedure, with checks and balances, for ordering goods and services (Chapter 4).

■ Have clear, supportive accountability systems for budget holders' use of money (Chapter 4).

■ Discourage as far as possible the practice of individuals making purchases on behalf of the school and then claiming money back. It's generally safer to use the school's ordering system.

■ Make sure that people always keep receipts for purchases made on behalf of the school and that these are kept as records.

■ However unpleasant it seems, ensure that all staff know that there is a procedure for whistle-blowing. Your LEA probably has a policy on this.

■ Never allow school money to pass through individuals' bank accounts.

■ Make sure that procedures for claiming any expenses, such as travel or subsistence costs, are run in accordance with clear guidelines and suitable receipts are requested.

■ Be particularly careful with petty cash, for example dinner or trip money. Store it in a safe and make sure that records of its collection and use are thorough (Chapter 11).

■ Carry out regular, thorough financial monitoring yourself and with your governors (Chapter 9).

■ Keep a Register of Business Interests for all governors and any staff who may make purchasing decisions, so that conflicts of interest can be avoided.

2 A checklist of routines and systems that need to be working effectively to satisfy audit requirements.

▓ Budget plans are clear and are submitted to the LEA punctually where necessary (Chapter 12).

▓ Monitoring returns that your LEA requires give a true picture and are returned on time (Chapter 9).

▓ There are clear plans for the use of any major budget surplus (rollover) or the elimination of any deficit (Chapter 1).

▓ Arrangements for delegation of financial authority to the head and staff are in place (Chapters 1 and 3).

▓ All the school's financial records, on paper and on computer, are up to date, correct and stored securely (Chapter 11).

▓ All the school's income is shown in the overall budget (Chapters 1 and 11).

▓ Tendering, contracting and purchasing procedures are sound and applied correctly (Chapters 4 and 6).

▓ The school evaluates itself using Best Value principles (Chapter 14).

▓ Earmarked funds are used for their intended purposes (Chapters 5 and 6).

▓ Spending is in accordance with the school's strategic plans (Chapters 6 and 8).

▓ Virements are used appropriately and records are kept (Chapter 10).

▓ VAT records are correctly maintained (Chapter 11).

▓ An up-to-date asset register, or inventory of property, is maintained.

▓ Any necessary records of dinner money, including free school meal payments, are up to date and correct.

• All computer software used in school is correctly licensed and the licences are available.

▓ School pupil registers are accurately kept and PLASC (annual headcount) returns are correct and agree with the registers.

▓ Previous audit recommendations have been acted upon.

> **Audit is mainly about financial management but can include other things – for example, maintenance of pupil registers – as this checklist shows.**

In summary

Audit is perhaps best seen as a necessary evil. Of course it's essential to ensure public money is being properly spent. But at the same time auditors are not concerned with educational outcomes, which are our business. Because acting upon audit recommendations can take us away from our main tasks as heads, and be a bit uncomfortable, it's better to make sure that the right procedures are in place before the auditors descend.

▶ Next step

Following the guidance in this book should prepare you for the financial management aspects of audit. Look through the checklists and use the chapters to which they refer, along with guidance from your LEA, to help you if you feel any remedial action may be needed.

Appendix: MIS checklist

A computerised financial management system will make short work of a number of tasks that can otherwise be quite time-consuming. This is particularly true if your system has data links to your LEA's financial systems.

If you are auditing your current system or looking to upgrade to a new one, the following checklist will help you.

A good financial management system will

▨ allow a list of suppliers and debtors to be defined

▨ enable orders, invoices and credit notes to be entered for suppliers and invoices, receipts, credit notes and write-offs for debtors

▨ offer reconciliation facilities against the bank account and to central accounting systems

▨ provide a petty cash facility for disbursements

▨ allow customised reports to be written for senior management and governing bodies

▨ calculate salary projections from contract details held in personnel data

▨ allocate user names and passwords to limit access to stored information

▨ use student data to estimate next year's funding

▨ generate cost centre budgets from existing budgets – these can be adjusted to reflect changing priorities in the school

▨ permit 'what if' scenarios to be generated

▨ reduce workload by ensuring you enter data only once.

Where to find out more

Useful websites

www.dfes.gov.uk/vfm

The site of the DfES Value for Money unit gives specific guidance for schools about Best Value as well as downloads of relevant publications.

www.audit-commission.gov.uk

Provides information about Best Value and, in its publications section, some Best Value inspection reports for education providers, especially LEA services, as well as many others. The financial benchmarking tools for schools, mentioned in Chapter 13, can be also be accessed from this site.

www.bestvalueinspections.gov.uk

Gives details of how the Audit Commission inspects Best Value. Schools are not subject to these inspections but the site explains the philosophy.

www.idea.gov.uk/bestvalue/

In-depth articles and ideas about good practice in Best Value and how to carry out Best Value reviews. Detailed, but not geared particularly to the education sector.

Publications

Ofsted (1999) *Handbook for Inspecting Primary and Nursery Schools*. London: The Stationery Office.

DfES/Ofsted (2002) *Best Value in Schools*. DfES Publication Ref. DfES/0090/2002.